Shellcraft Animals

Patricia Pope

GREATOUTDOORS PUBLISHING CO.
4747 TWENTY-EIGHTH STREET NORTH
ST. PETERSBURG, FLORIDA 33714

REPRINTED
June 1975, March 1976, July 1977, April, 1978
Jan. 1979, Nov. 1979, Aug. 1980, March, 1981

Library of Congress Cataloging in Publication Data
Pope, Patricia E.   1949-
    Shellcraft animals.

    1. Shellcraft. I. Title.
TT862.P66   745.55   75-15906
ISBN 0-8200-0507-x

Contents

Shell Identification

Auger Shells
¾ - 5"

Atlantic Bulla or Bubble Shell
½ - ¾"

Cap Shell
1¼"

Cerithium
½"

Ribbed Clam or Unequal Ark
½ - 1¼"

Smooth Clam or Smooth Lucine
½ - 1¼"

Coquina
¼ - ½"

Razor Clam
1¼"

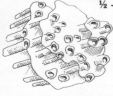

Organ Pipe Coral Tubes ¼ - ½"

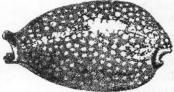

Atlantic Deer Cowrie
2 - 4"

Gold Ring Cowrie
½ - 1¼"

Snake-head Cowrie
1 - 1¼"

Cup Shell
¼ - 1¼"

Dove Shell
¼ x ½"

Drill
1 - 1¼"

Dwarf Olive
½ - 1"

Jingle Shell
½ - 1", upper shell curved, lower shell flat

Job's Tears or Pointed Nut Clam
½ - ¾"

Limpet
1 - 1½"

Key-hole Limpet
1"

Marginella
¼ - ½"

Moon Snail
1"

Mussel
1 - 1¼"

Nerite
¾ - 1"

Zebra Nerite
¼ - ½"

Operculum
1¼"

Pen Shell
2 - 3"

Scallop
¾ - 2"

Slipper Shell
½ - 2"

Top Shell
¼"

Turban Shell or
Venetian Pearl
¼"

Turkey Wing
2 - 3"

Tusk Shell
2"

Worm Snail
2 - 4"

General Techniques

Once you enter the hobby of shellcraft, you'll be amazed at the pleasure it brings yc Shellcraft is easy, fun, and relaxing. It requires no special talent, no expensive tools, o big investment in time. Many of the animals in this book were made in less than t minutes. As soon as you've worked a little with shells and glue, you'll build up spee Then even the harder-looking animals are easy!

If you don't have all the right parts to make a particular animal, don't be afraid substitute. This is what will make your animal your own creation. It's also a good way use up all those bits and pieces of shells you've accumulated over those trips to t seashore. You can make a lot of these animals entirely from shell rubble you've pick up at the beach; all you need buy is glue and pipe cleaners.

Some of these animals stand on a scallop shell with the help of a pipe cleaner brace. T pipe cleaner is glued to the animal at one end, and the other end passed through a hc in the scallop shell and glued up against the underside of the shell. To punch the hole i scallop yourself, just place the scallop, curved inner surface up, against a block of woc Hold a large (2½'') nail on the spot where you want your hole. Tap the nail lightly wit hammer. It may take several taps to make the hole the size and shape you want.

When the time comes to paint your creatures, you can do it one of two ways. You c paint solid areas of color with a brush, or you can use an old toothbrush to create a fi mist of paint that will coat your animal with tiny droplets. The second method is call "spatter painting". If you'd like to try this technique, dip the toothbrush into so thinned paint. Tap the brush against the side of the container to remove excess pai Then hold the brush, bristles up, in one hand. Hold a spoon by the bowl in your otl hand, and draw the handle of the spoon against the bristles. This will make a fine spr of paint off the end of the toothbrush — perfect for giving a small animal a tinge of col If the spatters are too large, thin down your paint some more, and tap more paint off t brush when you first dip it.

Materials

Glue - "527". "Orinoco", or any
   brand made for shellcraft
Pipe cleaners
Moveable eyes
Small magnets
Scissors
Needlenose pliers
Tweezers

Small beads - ⅛'' to ⅜'' diameter
Florist's wire
Flat-bottomed rhinestones
Paints (acrylics are best; oils
    work well, too) in red, brown,
    white, black, green, orange,
    yellow, pink
Rubber bands

Goggle-eyed Lady Bug

Materials:

1 - 1" cowrie, any kind (body)

2 - ⅛" movable eyes

1 - ½" square magnet, or a small refrigerator magnet

Red, black paint

What To Do:

1. **Paint the body red,** and allow it to dry completely. If you'd like to speed drying, place the body in a sunny spot. Remember to paint the underneath edges of the cowrie; it's easy to miss these areas.

2. **Add ladybug markings** by painting a narrow black stripe down the center of the back, and 3 or 4 small dots on each side. Again, allow to dry.

3. **Paint the head and tail** tip by painting each end of the cowrie black. This will leave the central half of the body red with black spots.

4. **Glue the two goggle eyes** atop the black head. Try not to reposition the eyes too much — you may find the glue removes the head paint.

5. **Glue magnet** on bottom.

If you'd like to spatter-paint the body instead of painting it solid red, be sure your paint is thin enough to spatter easily. You may find it best to give the body two coats of thin spatter paint, about 15 minutes apart.

7

Baby Sea Turtle

Materials:
1 - 1¼" operculum (body)
4 - 1" purple dwarf olive shells (feet)
1 - ¾" Atlantic Bulla or bubble shell (head)
1 - ½" broken tip from an auger (tail)
   Black paint

What To Do:

1. **For the feet,** place the four olive shells in a circle, with the mouths of the shells pointing inwards.

2. **Now, the body:** place the operculum atop the olive shells — don't use any glue at this stage — and reposition the feet slightly until the operculum is held up securely.

3. **Lift off the operculum** and place a dab of glue on the upper surface of each foot.

4. **Put the body back** down atop the feet, and press down a little to seat the body firmly.

5. **Glue the head,** mouth-side of the bubble shell against the operculum, to the body.

6. **Glue the tail** on the opposite end so that the tail stands up perkily.

7. **Use a fine brush** and black ink to add eyes to the head.

For more color, you can also touch up the body with shades of brown or green paint.

Veil-tail Goldfish

Materials:

1 - 1¼" snakehead cowrie (body)

3 - ½" slipper shells (2 fins and upper half of tail)

1 - ¾" slipper shell (lower half of tail)

Black, white paint

What To Do:

1. **Make the tail:** glue the ¾" and one of the ½" slipper shells together at an angle, curved sides up. Allow 15 minutes to dry.

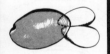

2. **Arrange the fins:** put the body down on a sheet of paper and trace around it. Put the body aside and arrange the fins so half of each slipper shell extends into the penciled body outline. Place a dot of glue on the top of each slipper shell, and place the body gently down on top. (The fins form a sort of tripod for the body to rest upon.) Make sure the narrow end of the cowrie is toward the tail.

3. **Touch up the body** with paint as desired — a golden yellow looks especially appropriate.

4. **For the finishing touch,** use a fine brush and white and black paint to add eye and gill slit.

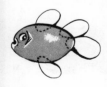

You may glue a small magnet to the bottom of the goldfish, so he can rest on your refrigerator. A strip of tape, folded sticky-side out, will enable you to perch your goldfish on mirrors, windows, cabinets, etc.

Magnetic Crab

Materials:
1 - 1" cowrie, any kind (body)
3 - 3" lengths of red pipe cleaner (legs)
2 - ½" gold ring cowries (clawtips)
1 - 1½ length of red pipe cleaner (claws)
1 - ½" square piece of plastic magnet
    red paint
    glue

What To Do:

1. **Paint the body.** Place the body cowrie mouth down and paint all exposed surfaces with red paint. Be sure to paint the partially exposed underside as well.
2. **Form legs.** Bend the last quarter-inch of the pipe cleaner legs over slightly. Do this for both ends of each of the three pieces of pipe cleaners. (The legs extend all the way across the body and down on each side. The bent area forms the feet.)
3. **Form claws.** Bend over the last quarter-inch of each end of the pipe cleaner used to form the claws. Slightly bow the middle of the pipe cleaner.
4. **Glue on claws.** Stick each bent end of the claw pipe cleaner into the opening at the wide end of the two small gold cowrie claws. (The cowrie shell is widest across where the opening is narrowest).
5. **Glue legs to body.** Hold the body, mouth up. Glue on the double legs, parallel to the mouth. Center the legs so an equal length extends on each side.
6. **Glue the claws in place.** The curved upper surface of the claw cowries should be down when the crab is turned right-side up. The mouth of these little cowries makes the claw look slightly open and ready to pinch.
7. **Attach magnet.** Glue the square magnet to the underside of the body, atop the legs you've already attached.
8. **Turn the crab right side up and attach the eyes.** Locate these eyes on the forward surface of the body, between the claws.

Apprehensive Dragonfly

Materials:
1 - 4" auger shell (body)
1 pair 3" pen shells (wings)
1 - 1" cowrie (head)
2 - ½" tube from organ pipe coral (mouth)
12" pipe cleaner, cut into 3 - 4" sections
   Black paint

What To Do:

1. **Give the dragonfly** his wings by gluing the pen shells, straight edges together, along the auger shell. The mouth of the auger should face down. The hind edges of the wings should be about ½" from the rear tip of the auger.

2. **Glue the cowrie head** to the large end of the auger, on the upper curve of the body.

3. **Bend the legs** into an "M" shape. Curve the descending middle of the "M".

4. **Add the legs** to the body by fitting the curve of the auger shell into the middle curve of the legs, and gluing into place.

5. **Glue the eyes** onto the upper curve of the head. The hinges of the cup shells should point to the upper outside edge of the face.

6. **Put the mouth** slightly below the eyes. If the mouth is angled a little bit, the dragonfly looks more doubting.

7. **Touch up the eyes** with the paint. You can make him look in any direction you wish.

Magnetic Mouse

Materials:
1 - 1" grey upper jingle shell (body)
1 - ½" grey cowrie (head)
2 - ⅓" cup shells (ears)
2" piece of rubber band
　Small refrigerator magnet
　Pink and black paints

What To Do:

1. **Glue the magnet** up inside the jingle shell. Depending on the depth of the jingle shell and the size of your magnet, you may wish to first glue in a shell fragment. The magnet can then be glued to this fragment, and then be able to hold the creature against a metal surface.

2. **Add the ears** to the head. Put a spot of glue on the underside of the wide end of the cowrie. Position the ears on this spot, so the curved inner surface of the ears will be toward the front.

3. **Position the tail** so it extends 1½" beyond the wide end of the jingle shell. If the tail is cut from the curved portion of the rubber band, this will give the tail an automatic curl.

4. **Put the head** on the mouse: glue the head and ears to the front of the jingle shell body. Remember to have the chin of the head touching the ground in front of the body.

5. **Touch up** with pink and black paints.

Butterfly

Materials:
- 2 - 1" upper jingle shells (upper wings)
- 2 - ¾" lower jingle shells (lower wings)
- 1 - 1" piece of pipe cleaner
- 1 - 2" scallop or clam shell (base)
- 1 - 1¼" razor clam (body)
- 2 - ¼" tubes from organ pipe coral (antennae)
  - Paints, if desired

What To Do:

1. **To make the left wings,** glue an upper jingle shell atop the lower jingle shell at the hinges. Move the shells around before the glue sets. You'll find that the dimple on the upper wing hinge will fit into a slight depression on the hinge of the lower wing. The right edge of the wing-pair should be straight — this is the edge that will support the body.

2. **Make the right wings** in the same way, but the left edge of the two shells should be straight.

3. **Glue the wings** together by overlapping and gluing the straight edges.

4. **Glue the folded strip** of pipe cleaner along the center seam of the wings.

5. **Glue the entire wing** and pipe cleaner assembly to the scallop shell base.

6. **Glue the antennae** to the razor clam body, just under the tip of the clam. Give this part ten minutes to dry; there isn't too much area on the curved surface of the antennae for the glue and razor clam to cling to.

7. **Glue the body** atop the wings and pipe cleaner base. Press down slightly after the glue has been applied, so the little fibers of the pipe cleaner can come into contact with the body.

8. **Touch up** with paints as desired.

Pink Piglet

Materials:

4 Job's tears, 2 small enough to fit
   inside the other 2 (ears)

1 - 1" gold ring cowrie (body)

1 - 1" length of florists wire (tail)

4 pink Venetian pearl shells (feet)

2 flat-bottomed rhinestones (eyes)

1 - ¼"pinkish cup shell (snout)

What To Do:

1. **Make the ears** by gluing the two smaller Job's tears inside the larger two.

2. **Put the feet on** the piglet by gluing the Venetian pearl shells on the bottom of the cowrie. The mouths of these pearl shells should fit against the cowrie.

3. **Curl the tail** by winding one end of the wire around a small nail until you have two or three coils.

4. **Attach the tail** to the piglet by gluing the free end of the tail into the narrow end of the cowrie.

5. **Add the nose** to the wide end of the body, about ⅛" above the bottom edge of the cowrie.

6. **Glue the eyes** above the snout, one on each side.

7. **Add the ears** to the top of the head, so the rounded bottom edge of each ear is just above an eye.

Quickly Duck

Materials:

1 - 1¼" gold ring cowrie (body)
1 - 1¼" ribbed clam (base)
2" pipe cleaner (support)
1 - ¾" gold ring cowrie (head)
2 - ¾" ribbed clams (wings)
4 coquinas (feet and beak)
   ribbed clam piece (hat)
   Black, white and yellow or pink paints.

What To Do:

1. **Glue the body** to the head, using the pipe cleaner as a support, pressed into the mouths of the cowries. Let a half-inch of the pipe cleaner extend out from the lower end of the body.
2. **Drill a hole** in the clam shell base with a nail.
3. **Push the free end** of the pipe cleaner into the hole in the clam shell base, and glue it up into place on the underside of the shell.
4. **Attach the wings** to the body with glue. The hinge edge of the wings should be toward the front.
5. **Put a narrow strip** of glue along the short edge near the hinge of two coquinas. Hold for a moment, until the glue gets sticky. Glue these two coquinas, short edges together, against the lower side of the head. If you move the beak shells around a little, you'll find a flat spot on the head shell where the coquinas can rest. Allow to dry.
6. **Give the duck** his hat. Glue the ribbed clam shell fragment to the top front of the head. Leave enough room between the lower edge of the hat and the beak to paint the eyes in later.
7. **Add the final two** coquinas to the base, as feet.
8. **Now paint on the eyes.** You'll find that a spot of white, allowed to dry, makes a good base for the addition of a black pupil a few minutes later.
9. **Touch up the duck** with yellow or pink paints. We used pink on our duck, to match the pink already in the coquina beak.

Happy-Go Monkey

Materials:
1 - 1" snakehead cowrie (body)
2 - ¾" scallop shells (head)
3 - ¼" cup shells (snout, ears)
12 inches of brown pipe cleaner, cut into
    lengths of 5, 4, and 3" (arms, legs, tail)
    black paint or ink (face)

What To Do:

1. **Form the head** by gluing the two ¾" scallop shells together.
2. **Make the arms** by folding the 5" length of pipe cleaner in half, and then bending up the last half inch for hands.
3. **Make the legs** the same way as the hands.
4. **Put the arms and legs in place** by inserting the folded middle into the mouth of the cowrie and gluing into place. Let dry a few minutes.
5. **Add tail** by gluing end of 3" pipe cleaner in cowrie mouth. Curl the end of the tail upward.
6. **Add snout** to face by gluing one cup shell against the lower hinge edge of the head.
7. **Add the ears** to the upper back surface of the head.
8. **Glue head to upper tip of cowrie body.** You may find the head is easier to glue on if you turn the head slightly to one side, so the tip of the cowrie fits between the hinges of the head scallop.
9. **Tint the head** and ears brown.
10. **Add a merry smile** by drawing a fine black line along one of the growth rings of the snout cup shell. Tip the hinge of the snout cup shell hinge with black for nose. Paint in eyes, just above the snout.

If you don't have colored pipe cleaners, you can tint white ones by stroking them lightly with an almost-dry paint brush. Tint hands and feet pink in the same way.

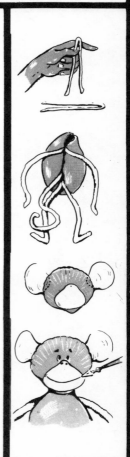

Dandie Dinmont Puppy

Materials:
1 pair 1¼" ribbed clams (body)
1 - 1" ribbed clam (base)
2 pair ¾" ribbed clams (head & muzzle)
2 - ½" ribbed clams (ears)
1" pipe cleaner
1 - ¼" diameter bead (dog tag)
    Black paint

What To Do:

1. **Glue the body together.** Hold the clam halves against each other with a rubber band while you're waiting for them to dry. Make the muzzle and head units in the same way.
2. **Attach the ears** by gluing the cupped side of two ½" ribbed clams against the upper outside edges of the head. The ears will dry in the correct position if you turn the head face downward; the head forms the center portion of a tripod, and the ears the other two legs.
3. **Glue the muzzle** to the head with glue so they form a "V" in side view. Before this joint dries completely, go onto the next step.
4. **Attach the head/muzzle** unit to the body. The joined edge of the body shells will fit into a small "V" formed by the joining of the head and muzzle.
5. **Glue the body and head** to the base. The hinge of the body shells should be to the lower right as the puppy faces you.
6. **Add the tail** by gluing the pipe cleaner along the lower left seam of the body clam shells. Be sure to leave the tail tip free, and put a bend in it.
7. **Paint black dot eyes** and a black dot nose on the face.
8. **Add bead** at neck.
9. **Tint the body** however you like. You can use any color, but if you used a colored pipe cleaner for the tail, you may want to match the color.

Southern Belle

Materials

1 - 1¼" scallop (base)
9 - 1" jingle shells (skirt)
1 - 1¼" jingle shell (bonnet)
1 - ½" cup shell (face)
3" pipe cleaner (arms)
2 - ¾" jingle shells (body)
    fragment of organ pipe coral
    black paint

What To Do:

1. **Make the skirt.** Place the scallop shell, curved surface down, and glue three of the skirt jingle shells over it. Spread the jingle shells out so they cover the scallop shell.
2. **Put on the second skirt layer.** Take three more jingle shells and glue them over the seams of the first layer.
3. **Add the final layer** of jingle shells, but this time, draw the center junction of these three upwards, so the top comes to a point.
4. **Glue the two body** jingle shells together.
5. **Fit the face cup** shell into the hinge area of the bonnet jingle shell, and glue it in place.
6. **Put the body** on the skirt by gluing the hinge edge of the body jingle shells to the peak of the skirt. This will be easier if you can brace the body against something, like a toaster, until the glue has a chance to set.
7. **After the body** is secure, glue the head and bonnet on top. Angle the head downwards slightly so the Southern Belle looks demure.
8. **Bend the two ends** of the pipe cleaner until they meet in the middle. Then bend the pipe cleaner in the middle, until you have what looks like a fat "V". These will be the arms.
9. **Glue the arms** to the body, and glue the organ pipe coral fragment to the apex of the "V", at the waist.
10. **Give the Belle** a smile and eyes with black paint or India ink.

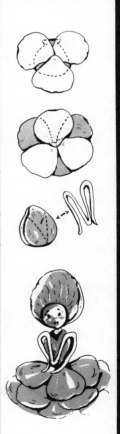

Military Macaw

Materials:

1 - 2" scallop shell with hole (base)
1 - 3" length of pipe cleaner (stand)
1 - ¾" nerite (head)
1 - ½" slipper shell (beak)
1 - 1" mussel shell (tail)
1 - 2" wood sliver; a wooden match
    will work (perch)
    Red, yellow, blue and green paints

What To Do:

1. **Begin the stand:** stick ½" of the stand pipe cleaner into the hole in the scallop shell base. Fold the pipe cleaner up against the underside of the scallop shell, and glue it into place.

2. **Glue the head** to the tip of the body. Allow to dry.

3. **Add the tail:** turn the head and body unit over, so the bird is resting stomach-up. Dab glue on the hinge end of the tail mussel, and glue it on the tip of the cowrie opposite the head. Prop the tail up against another shell or the edge of a book, so it can dry at the correct angle.

4. **Add the beak:** glue the small slipper shell, rounded tip toward the top, to the macaw's head. The end of the beak should project down, past the underside of the head — like a real macaw's beak.

5. **Put the macaw on his perch:** glue the wood sliver across the base of the cowrie. Leave a narrow portion of the cowrie mouth open between the perch and the tail. This is where the stand will go.

6. **Stand the parrot upright:** thread about half an inch of glue-spotted stand into the small opening at the tail of the macaw.

7. **Color the macaw** with red, blue, green and yellow paints using fine brushes.

Look at the assorted bird books to see what other colors macaws are, and paint other macaw versions to match.

Donkey Hotey

Materials:

1 - 1¼" cowrie (head)	2 - 2" slipper shells (body)
1 - ⅓" marginella (mouth)	8 - ¾" augers (legs)
2 - ½" dove shells (ears)	4 - ¾" slipper shells (feet)
1 - ¾" nerite (neck)	2 - ⅛" pipe cleaner (eyes)
	1 - 1" pipe cleaner (tail)

What ToDo:

1. **Make the body** by gluing the two large slipper shells together, hinge to hinge.

2. **Add the mouth** to the head: glue the apex of the marginella to the narrow end of the head cowrie, about ¼" back from the front edge of the cowrie.

3. **Add the dove shells** to the rear upper surface of the head to form the ears. Add eyes.

4. **Attach the neck nerite** to the end of the head cowrie, just below the ears. You'll find that the end of the cowrie fits neatly into the mouth of the nerite.

5. **Make a leg** by overlapping and gluing the tips of two ¾" augers. Make the other three legs in the same way. Line the legs up as you make them so you can make them the same length.

6. **Shoe the donkey** by gluing an end of each leg against the hinge edge of each of the ¾" slipper shells.

7. **Stand the donkey upright** by gluing the legs to the body. You'll find that the seam between the two slipper shells that form the body makes a good spot to anchor the legs.

8. **Glue the head** and neck to the front edge of the body. If you put a dab of glue on the right spot on the body,   and let it dry until it is very tacky, the gluing process will be easier.

9. **Add the tail** to the rear edge of the body.

Banjo Frog

Materials:

1 - 1¼" nutmeg (body)

3 - 1" jingle shells (banjo and head)

4 - 1" purple dwarf olives (legs)

2 - 1" limpets (feet)

2 - ¼" zebra nerites (eyes)

1 - 2" tusk shell (banjo neck)

2 - ⅓" flat pieces of organ pipe coral (hands)

6" pipe cleaner, cut into lengths of
   5" and 1"

What To Do:

1. **Form a leg** by gluing two dwarf olives together, tip to tip. Make the second leg the same way.
2. **Make the banjo:** glue the open end of the tusk shell to the hinge curve of a jingle shell.
3. **To make the smiling head,** overlap the final two jingle shells and glue together. Make sure the top jingle shell sits slightly behind the lower shell; this is what makes the mouth.
4. **Bend the 1" piece** of pipe cleaner into a "V". Dip each end into glue and fit it into the end of a leg.
5. **Put a spot of glue** on the top of each limpet. Fit the free end of a leg atop each limpet.
6. **Glue the legs** on the mouth edge of the body nutmeg. Stand this body/legs unit upright and make any needed adjustments in the position of the legs so the frog can stand upright.
7. **Bend the 5" pipe cleaner** into a "U" shape. Bend the straight arms of the "U" again to form elbows. Glue the flat pieces of coral on the ends of the arms to form hands.
8. **Add the two eyes** to the top of the head.
9. **Glue the head** to the body.
10. **Glue the arms** on the body.
11. **Glue the banjo** in place against the front of the body and the raised left hand.

Pea Soup Frog

Materials:
- 2 - 1" smooth clams (head)
- 1 - 1" Moon Snail (body)
- 2 - ½" smooth clams (feet)
- 2 - ⅜" diameter beads (eyes)
    - Olive green, red, and black paints

What To Do:
1. **Glue the head together,** with the upper shell overlapping the rear of the lower shell about ¼". Apply the glue to the back rim of the lower shell, and to the midpoint on each side of the upper shell. Overlapping the head shells in this way gives the frog an open mouth.
2. **Attach the body** to the feet by gluing the moon snail, mouth down, atop the curved surface of each foot.
3. **Add the head** to the body, directly over the feet.
4. **Glue the eyes** atop the head. Align the bead/eyes so the holes go from side to side, and won't be in the way when you paint the eyes.
5. **Paint the body,** head, and eyes with a spatter of green paint.
6. **Paint the eyes** with a dot of black paint on the upper surface, so the frog is looking upwards.
7. **Add a tongue** with a dab of red paint inside the lower edge of the mouth.

Big Limpet Crab

Materials:

21" of pipe cleaner, cut into
- 4 - 3" lengths (legs)
- 2 - 2" lengths (legs)
- 2 - 1" lengths (eyestalks)
- 2 - 1½" lengths (claw arms)

2 - ¾" cowries (claws)

2 - ¼" zebra nerites (eyes)

1 - 1½" limpet (body)

What To Do:

1. **Hold the limpet,** concave side up, and glue in three legs along each end of the limpet. The legs will stick out like sticks — but we'll correct that later.

2. **Glue in the claw arms,** just in front of the legs. Use plenty of glue, prop the limpet up so the legs won't fall out, and give it fifteen minutes to dry.

3. **After the legs** have dried, glue the eyestalks in the center front of the limpet. Let them dry five minutes, and then bend them so they stand vertically when you flip the crab over.

4. **Now the crab** is right-side up, bend elbows in the claw arms.

5. **Dab glue on the ends** of the claw arms, and insert them into the cowries you're using for claws. Twist these cowries slightly, so the mouth is toward the front of the crab.

6. **Bend the legs** so the body is close to the ground, and the knees on a level with the peak of the body. You may have to try several ways of bending, before the crab stands straight on his feet and does not wobble.

7. **Touch up** the crab with paint as desired.

Puff
the Magic Dragon

Materials:

6 - ½" augers (legs and arms) 1 - 1" drill (head)
2 - 1¼" augers (tail and neck) 2 - ¾" limpets (hands)
1 - 1¼" drill or nutmeg (body) 2 - 1" limpets (feet)
1 - 1" stalked barnacle (crest) Needlenose pliers
2 - ¼" dove shells (eyes) Paints

What To Do:
1. **Modify the head.** Hold the head shell in one hand, and use the pliers to pinch ⅛" off the apex of the shell. Then break tiny pieces off the edge of the mouth until you can see the central whorl from the side.
2. **Make the arms** by gluing the mouth of one ½" auger over the tip of a second auger. Angle the two augers at about a 90° angle, so the arm looks bent at the elbow. Make both arms this way.
3. **Put the legs on** the feet by gluing the tip of two more ½" augers onto the peaks of the feet limpets. You may find it easier gluing if you use your pliers to break off a tiny part of the auger tip (about ⅛"); the glue will be better able to hold.
4. **Glue the hands** to the tips of the arms. The tip of the forearm auger should lie along the inside of the limpet, with the very tip of the auger in the center of the limpet.
5. **Use the pliers again** to snip ⅛" off the apex of the body drill. This will make it easier to add the head later.
6. **Glue the body** to the legs. Position the legs so the body will balance upright.
7. **Put a spot** of glue on the tail auger, and fit the tail into place.
8. **Glue the mouth** of the neck auger to the free tip of the body shell.

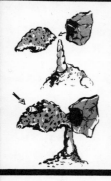

9. **Attach the arms** to the body, so it looks as though the dragon is holding his arms out in front of him.
10. **Place a dab** of glue on the broken apex of the head auger. Press the head onto the neck auger.
11. **While the glue** on the head and neck is still tacky, add the crest to the back of the head.
12. **Glue the eyes** to the front of the head.
13. **Add a touch** of red to the open mouth, and paint the eyes.

Florida Lobster

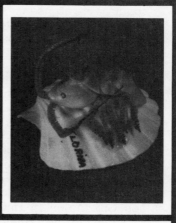

Materials:

19 ½" orange pipe cleaner, cut into
    1½", 6" and 4 - 3" lengths
1 - 2½" scallop shell
1 - ¾" gold cowrie
4 - ¾" coquina shells
1 - ½" cup shell
    Matches; black and orange paints
    Toothbrush for splatter painting

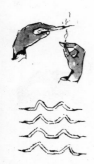

What To Do:
1. **Taper the legs.** Pick up one of the 3" leg lengths, and touch a lighted match to both ends. The pipe cleaner will catch fire and burn with small flame. Let half-inch of each end burn, then blow out the flame. If you're hesitant about lighting the pipe cleaner, try it over the sink first. If you drop the lighted pipe cleaner, no harm is done.
2. **Bend the legs.** Take one of the tapered legs and bend it into a sort of an "M", as shown.
3. **Taper the feelers.** Burn the two ends of the 6" length of pipe cleaner as you did the legs, but this time burn the first inch of each end. Fold the pipe cleaner in half, to yield a pair of feelers, nicely tapered.

4. **Connect the tail** and head. Glue the cup shell to one end of the 1½" pipe cleaner. Thread and glue the gold ring cowrie onto the other end, leaving the middle ½" of the pipe cleaner bare. On this half-inch, you'll form the back.

5. **Form the back.** Starting with the head, overlap and glue the coquinas in a line to the tail. One end of the coquina will be anchored to the shell in front of it; the other end will be anchored to the pipe cleaner underneath it. Make sure the hinges of the coquinas are aligned the same way.

6. **Paint the body.** Use the toothbrush, thinned paint, and the handle of a spoon to spatter the body. Concentrate the coloring on the rear of the lobster. Allow to dry.

7. **Attach the legs.** Turn the lobster upside down, and thread glue along the pipe cleaner. Press the flattened middle of each leg-pair across the spine.

8. **Put on the feelers.** Put a spot of glue under the front edge of the cowrie head, and press the doubled middle portion of the feelers against the glue.

9. **Attach the lobster** to the scallop base. Put a touch of glue on the underside of each foot. Thread a strip of glue along the pipe cleaner backbone-leg junction. Give the lobster a few moments for the glue to set. Then turn the lobster rightside up, and position him atop the scallop shell base. He should be facing the scallop shell hinge. Press down slightly, so the glue has a chance to bond to the shell.

10. **Add the eyes** with black paint and a fine brush. You may want to touch up the edges of the shells with black, as well.

11. **Bend the feelers** upwards for a perky look. The lobster can be used for a place-card holder if the feelers are first bent downwards, and the tips flexed upwards. The place-card will then rest atop the feelers.

You can add a personal touch by printing a word or short message on the scallop shell base. Our example says "Florida"; you could put a favorite person's name. Position the lobster on his base so you have room for your message.

Bald Eagle

Materials:

1 - 1"auger (beak)
1 - 1¼" cap shell (head)
1 - 3" cowrie (body)
1 - 2½" clam shell (base)
1 - 2½" section worm snail or wooden twig
   (branch)
2 - 2½" mussel shells (wings)
   Brown, black, yellow paint

What To Do:

1. **Glue the beak** on the head: glue the auger shell (or tip of broken auger shell) to the peak of the cap shell. Have the auger shell extend out on a horizontal line from the cup shell.

2. **Glue the head** on the end of the cowrie body. Angle the head so it slants back slightly from the underside of the cowrie.

3. **Now the body** goes on the base: glue the free end of the body onto the hinge edge of the base shell. The eagle will look as though he were teetering on the back edge of the shell.

4. **Dab glue along** the underside of the worm snail shell, and glue the shell atop the base shell, against the body of the eagle.

5. **Glue the wings** on the body. If the wings are large enough, the tips can rest on the ground. This forms a tripod with the base, and your shellcraft animal is sturdier.

6. **Paint the body** with brown paint, making sure the head is left white.

7. **Using the fine tip** of your brown paintbrush, add the eagle's feet to the branch in front of his body.

8. **Paint the beak** yellow, and put eyes on each side of the head.

27

Japanese Squirrel

Materials:
2 - 1¼" limpets (body)
1 - 1" limpet (hat)
1 pair - 1¼" mussels (tail)
2 - ½" marginellas (paws)
2 - ½" cerithium shells (feet)
1 - 1" gold ring cowrie (head)

What To Do:
1. **First, make the tail** by gluing the mussel shells together edge to edge.
2. **Form the body.** Squeeze a short strip of glue along the wide end of each large limpet, and press the limpets together. Leave the unglued end open about ¼", so the limpets form an inverted "V". Hold the limpets until the glue gets tacky, about 2minutes.
3. **Dab the feet** with glue and insert them in the space left open between the two limpets. Push the two limpets together until the feet are held in place. The cerithium mouths should be toward the inside of the limpet body. A rubber band can be used to hold the body and feet in place until the glue dries.
4. **Put the hat atop** the head: glue the small limpet on the wide end of the gold-ring cowrie.
5. **Give the squirrel** his paws. Glue one marginella on each side of the body, about 2/3 of the way up.
6. **Put a spot** of glue atop the junction of the body limpets. Give the glue a moment to get sticky, and press the head gently into place. Slant the head slightly toward the front.
7. **Glue the tail** on so the curved edge forms the third leg of a tripod with the feet.
8. **Give the squirrel** a face by painting the front of the face reddish-brown. When this dries, add black and white paint for the eyes.

28

Little Brown Wren

1 - 1¼" snake-head cowrie (body)
9 - ¾" mussels (4 pair for feet, wings, and
    back feathers; 1 extra for tail)
1 - ¾" nerite (head)
1 - ¼" turban shell (beak)

What To Do:

1. **For the feet,** line up a pair of mussels so the straight sides are together. Glue lightly along this center seam.
2. **Add the body:** glue cowrie, curved side down, atop the feet. Tilt the cowrie a little so the end close to the rear of the feet is lower.
3. **Give the wren his beak.** Glue the beak atop the head, a little toward the rear of the shell (the rear of the shell will be the front of the head).
4. **The back feathers** are made by gluing a pair of mussels atop the back edge of the cowrie. The straight edges of the mussels should be together and fit down into the mouth of the cowrie.
5. **Glue the second set** of back feathers atop the first set. Position this second set so about ¼" of the lower back feathers are left exposed.
6. **Make the wings** by adding another pair of mussels, one on each side of the body. Glue the curved front edge to the body; the hinge edge should point upwards and toward the tail. The hinges should touch over the back.
7. **Add the head** to the body. The front edge of the head should be even with the edge of the body; the mouth of the nerite should be over the middle of the body.
8. **Add the single tail** by gluing the extra mussel, hinge down, to the junction of the four back feathers. Put a dab of glue on the center of the tail, and push it forward slightly, until it touches the wing feathers.
9. **Paint an eye** on each side of the head.

Perky Penguin

Materials:
1 - 1" keyhole limpet (base)
1 - ¾" gold ring cowrie (body)
1 - ⅓" marginella shell (head)
2 - ¼" limpet shells (wings)
   ½ pipe cleaner (support)
   Black, white, and orange paints.

What To Do:

1. **Stand the body upright** by threading one end of the pipe cleaner through the hole in the limpet base, and the other end into the wide end of the cowrie (where the mouth is narrowest). Glue in place so the cowrie is held upright on the base.

2. **Make the penguin flap his wings** by gluing the short side of the small limpets against each side of the narrow end of the body. If the penguin is lying on his back, the wings will be supported and dry in place.

3. **Put a dab of glue** on the very tip of the body and on the apex of the head shell. Wait for 30 seconds or until the glue becomes very tacky, then place the head atop the body. Put the head on at an angle, so it seems as though the bird is looking directly at you.

4. **Paint the tummy** and the head of the penguin white.

5. **Paint the wings,** back, side and top of head black.

6. **Paint the beak**.

Kit and Capoodle

Materials:

1 - 1" gold ring cowrie (body)
1 - ¾" gold ring cowrie (forebody)
1 - ½" gold ring cowrie, filed
    in half crossways (muzzle)
1 - 1" pipe cleaner (tail)
4 - ¾" ribbed clams (head & ears)
1 - ½" ribbed clam (topknot)
1 - ¼" top shell (hairbow)
1 - ⅛" glass bead (dog tag)
    Wooden base, 1½" x 2"

What To Do:

1. **Glue the head together,** using two of the ¾" ribbed clams.
2. **Attach the muzzle** to the head, being careful to center it on the lower curved portion near the hinge.
3. **Add the ears,** hinge forewards, to each side of the head. The hinge of each ear shell should fit against the muzzle.
4. **Glue the topknot** to the top of the head, with the hinge of the topknot shell just meeting the muzzle on the top.
5. **Put the body** and forebody together with glue, so the front edge of the forebody rests on the ground, and the rear half is elevated on the body.
6. **Dip one end** of the tail in glue, and press it into place on the free end of the body. Curve the other end upwards.
7. **Dab glue** on the underside of both the forebody and body, and press them lightly into place on the base.
8. **Glue the head** to the curved portion of the forebody directly above the forebody-body joint.
9. **Add the hairbow** to the top of the head.
10. **Paint** on the eyes.
11. **Place the dog tag** on the neck, just under the muzzle.

Cock O' the Rock

Materials:
one pair ½" ribbed clams (head)
1 - ½" ribbed clam (neck)
1 - 1" ribbed clam (base)
1 - 1" length pipe cleaner (support)
1 - 1" cowrie, any kind (body)
2 - ¾" ribbed clams (wings)
2 - ½" coquinas (feet)
paints

What To Do:

1. **Make the head** by gluing shut the pair of ribbed clams. A bit of glue-soaked cotton in the center will help hold them together.

2. **Glue the head** to the neck, so the head stands vertically. The hinge edges of the head and neck should be toward the back.

3. **For the base,** bore a small hole in the center of the base clam, where you want your bird to sit. Insert half the pipe cleaner in this hole. Bend it up against the underside of the shell, and glue in place.

4. **Stand the body upright:** dab glue on the upper end of the pipe cleaner. Insert this end into the wide end of the body cowrie (where the mouth is narrowest), so the body stands upright on the base.

5. **Attach the wings** to the body by gluing the hinge edge of the 1" ribbed clams along the mouth opening of the body cowrie.

6. **Add the head** and neck to the top of the body while the glue holding the wings is still tacky. An extra dab of glue in the undercurve of the neck will help the neck and head stay in place more securely.

7. **Attach the coquina feet** to the base shell, just in front of the cowrie body.

8. **Paint** on the eyes and mouth.

9. **Touch up** the figure with paint as desired. The actual Cock O' the Rock is red-orange all over.